BENAZIR
BHUTTO

PAKISTANI PRIME MINISTER AND ACTIVIST

BENAZIR
BHUTTO
PAKISTANI PRIME MINISTER AND ACTIVIST

by Mary Englar

Content Adviser: Keith Snodgrass, Associate Director and
Outreach Coordinator, South Asia Center, Jackson School of
International Studies, University of Washington, Seattle

Reading Adviser: Susan Kesselring, M.A.,
Literacy Educator, Rosemount–Apple Valley–Eagan
(Minnesota) School District

COMPASS POINT BOOKS  MINNEAPOLIS, MINNESOTA

Compass Point Books
3109 West 50th Street, #115
Minneapolis, MN 55410

Visit Compass Point Books on the Internet at *www.compasspointbooks.com*
or e-mail your request to *custserv@compasspointbooks.com*

Editor: Jennifer VanVoorst
Page Production: Heather Griffin
Photo Researchers: Bobbie Nuytten and Marcie C. Spence
Cartographer: XNR Productions, Inc.
Library Consultant: Kathleen Baxter

Art Director: Jaime Martens
Creative Director: Keith Griffin
Editorial Director: Carol Jones
Managing Editor: Catherine Neitge

Library of Congress Cataloging-in-Publication Data
Englar, Mary.
  Benazir Bhutto: Pakistani prime minister and activist / by Mary Englar.
    p. cm. — (Signature lives)
  Includes bibliographical references and index.
  ISBN-13: 978-0-7565-1578-2 (hardcover)
  ISBN-10: 0-7565-1578-5 (hardcover)
  ISBN-13: 978-0-7565-1798-4 (paperback)
  ISBN-10: 0-7565-1798-2 (paperback)
  1. Bhutto, Benazir—Juvenile literature. 2. Prime ministers—Pakistan—
Biography—Juvenile literature. I. Title. II. Series.
  DS385.B44E54 2006
  954.9105'2092—dc22   2005025094

MODERN WORLD

From 1900 to the present day, humanity and the world have undergone major changes. New political ideas resulted in worldwide wars. Fascism and communism divided some countries, and democracy brought others together. Drastic shifts in theories and practice tested the standards of personal freedoms and religious conventions as well as science, technology, and industry. These changes have created a need for world policies and an understanding of international relations. The new mind-set of the modern world includes a focus on humanitarianism and the belief that a global economy has made the world a more connected place.

Table of Contents

THE FIRST WOMAN
PRIME MINISTER OF PAKISTAN 9

A PAKISTANI GIRLHOOD 15

A GROWING AWARENESS 25

TO COLLEGE AND BACK 33

THE PRISON YEARS 47

LIVING IN EXILE 59

RETURN TO PAKISTAN 69

PRIME MINISTER
BENAZIR BHUTTO 77

LOOKING FORWARD,
LOOKING BACK 89

LIFE AND TIMES 96
LIFE AT A GLANCE 102
ADDITIONAL RESOURCES 103
GLOSSARY 105
SOURCE NOTES 106
SELECT BIBLIOGRAPHY 108
INDEX 109
IMAGE CREDITS 112

1 First Woman Prime Minister of Pakistan

❦

Dressed in a green silk *shalwar kamiz*, with a white scarf covering her dark hair, Benazir Bhutto climbed the wide steps at the presidential palace in Islamabad, Pakistan, and entered the audience hall on the arm of the president. Guards dressed in white uniforms and gold turbans escorted the pair. On either side of the red carpet, army generals, Islamic leaders, and politicians watched as Bhutto approached the front.

Her political party, the Pakistan People's Party (PPP), had won the first free elections in 11 years. Now, on December 2, 1988, she stood before supporters and critics alike to be sworn in as prime minister of the Islamic Republic of Pakistan. When she placed her hand on the Pakistani constitution

Benazir Bhutto spoke to reporters following her historic election as the first female prime minister of Pakistan.

Bhutto's groundbreaking election as prime minister of Pakistan has opened doors for many women in politics. South Asia, a region of the world to which Pakistan belongs, has become known for its women in leadership positions within the government.

to take her oath of office, Bhutto became not only her country's first woman prime minister, but also the first woman in the world to lead an Islamic nation.

At the time of her inauguration, Bhutto was 35 years old. Married for only a year, she had given birth to her first child just two months before the election. She had never run for political office before, and she had never planned to become a politician. Though she had grown up in a political family, as the daughter of Pakistan's first democratically elected leader, she recalled, "When I was a child, there were many attempts on my father's life. Politics scared me." She knew that in Pakistan, political beliefs might lead to death. She had already spent more than seven years in prison or under house arrest for her active support of democratic elections. But when the Pakistan People's Party asked her to run for office, she felt a duty to both her father and her country to accept the challenge.

For many in Pakistan, Benazir Bhutto reminded them of her father, Zulfikar Ali Bhutto, who had founded the PPP and served as Pakistan's leader. The connection reminded them of a time in their history when they felt hopeful for their young

Bhutto's father was her hero, as well as being a hero to many Pakistanis.

nation. But for her critics, Bhutto was a threat to their Islamic values. In Pakistan's conservative Islamic society, women did not leave the house without an escort. The idea of a woman prime minister went against their traditional beliefs.

But Bhutto came from a family that had long challenged tradition. Her father broke with many

Bhutto speaks before many important international organizations about issues of democracy and human rights.

family traditions when he went to the United States for college. He married for love, and he encouraged his children—both sons and daughters—to get a good education. Bhutto remembers her father telling her as a child, "Boys and girls are equal. I want my daughter[s] to have the same opportunities." Her father always believed she could do anything she wanted. She did not let him down.

Today, Benazir Bhutto speaks out for democracy and human rights around the world. Though she lives in exile, Bhutto continues to fight for the right of Pakistanis to elect their government leaders, as well as for her right to return to Pakistan to run for political office. Driven by strong ideals and her family legacy, she fights for the rights of Pakistani women, political prisoners, and for laws that respect human rights.

Additional opposition to Benazir Bhutto resulted from her interest in reducing the role of the military in government. The military had long played a very important role in Pakistan's government, and the military naturally resisted anyone or anything that would limit its power.

2 A PAKISTANI GIRLHOOD

❧❧

When Benazir Bhutto was born on June 21, 1953, Pakistan was a young country. It was created just six years earlier, after the British colony of India was divided into the two independent countries of India and Pakistan. At that time, Mohammed Ali Jinnah, president of the Muslim League, fought for the rights of India's Muslims to rule themselves. He disagreed with plans for a united government for all of India and pushed for the creation of Pakistan, a homeland for India's Muslims.

In 1947, Pakistan officially became an independent country, but it was divided into two sections. These sections, called East Pakistan and West Pakistan, were separated by 1,000 miles (1,600 kilometers), as well as vast differences in culture and language.

Today, Karachi is a bustling city with a population of 130 million.

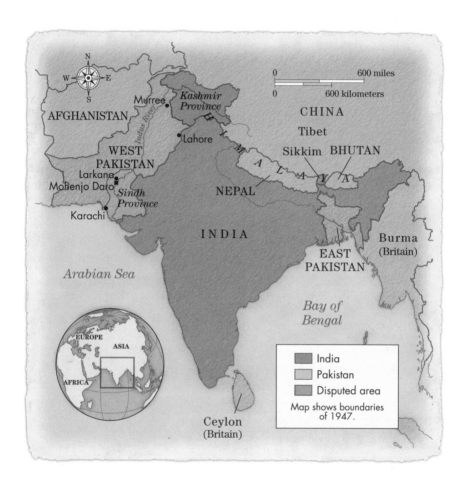

Bhutto was born in the West Pakistan city of Karachi, a large seaport on the Arabian Sea and the capital of Pakistan at the time. Her father, Zulfikar Ali Bhutto, had broken with the tradition of an arranged marriage. Instead, he married her mother, Nusrat Ispahani, for love.

But Zulfikar had been married once before. At age 13, his family had arranged for him to marry his cousin Amir. The marriage was a business arrangement to make sure their valuable lands stayed in the Bhutto family. But young Zulfikar did not want to marry, and he never lived with his first wife. She returned to her family, and Zulfikar stayed with his parents.

When Benazir's father went away to study at the University of California at Berkeley and later to Oxford University in England, he witnessed the contributions women made to western society. He became convinced that Pakistani women needed more freedom. In 1951, he married Nusrat Ispahani. Nusrat came from Iran, and she did not grow up with the same laws for women. She had never worn a veil, she drove her own car, and she had gone to college. In contrast, traditional Pakistani women were rarely educated, and after marriage, they lived separately from the men in the private women's quarters of their houses.

Benazir was the oldest of the Bhutto children. Her

> *In some Muslim families in Pakistan, men and women are kept separated. This tradition is called purdah. Zulfikar Bhutto's family practiced purdah. The women of the family lived in a separate part of the house from the men. Women rarely left the house, and when they did, they wore a veil. Benazir remembers that her mother wore a veil to respect the Bhutto family traditions. When Benazir was 12, her mother made her put on a veil for a train ride to the family farm. But Benazir's father did not agree, and said Benazir did not have to wear a veil.*

parents nicknamed her "Pinkie," because as a baby her skin was so rosy. Her brother Mir Murtaza was born in 1954, followed by a sister, Sanam, in 1957, and another brother, Shah Nawaz, in 1958.

Though the family lived in Karachi, the Bhuttos spent most holidays at the family farm, Al-Murtaza, north of Karachi. The farm covered more than 10,000 acres (4,047 hectares) along the banks of the Indus River, in the province of Sindh. Benazir's father and his sisters were born at Al-Murtaza, and many photographs of the family's ancestors lined the walls of the home. In her autobiography, *Daughter of Destiny*, Bhutto wrote:

> *Al-Murtaza was the heart of our family, the house to which we always returned from the four corners of the earth to pass our winter vacations, to celebrate Eid [a Muslim holiday] at the end of the holy month of Ramazan [Ramadan], as well as my father's birthday.*

Not far from Al-Murtaza stand the ruins of the ancient city of Mohenjo-daro. More than 4,500 years ago, it had been a bustling city of 50,000. As a child, Benazir misunderstood the name of this ancient place. She thought it was called Munj Jo Dero. In her native language of Sindhi, this translated as "my place." She believed that the archeological site was the home of

her ancestors—and no wonder: The front door of Al-Murtaza was decorated with blue and white tiles that showed men and women of Mohenjo-daro at work. She later wrote:

Mohenjo-daro is a city of great historic significance to Pakistan.

> *My brothers, sisters, and I took great pride that we had been raised in the shadow of Mohenjo-daro, that we lived on the bank of the Indus [River], which had been bringing life to the land since the beginning of time. In no other place did we feel such continuity with the past.*

When it came time for Benazir to begin her education, her family's wealth made it possible for her to attend the best schools. In Pakistan, these schools were private and often run by foreigners. Benazir began nursery school at 3 and started elementary school at a Catholic private school, the Convent of Jesus and Mary, when she was 5. The school was just down the road from Benazir's house in Karachi. The Catholic nuns taught their students in English.

Benazir's mother was a Shiite Muslim, as are most of the people in Iran. The Shiite Muslims are a minority of Muslims worldwide. The majority of Muslims belong to the Sunni tradition. Benazir's father was a Sunni Muslim. Though there are some differences between the two traditions, Benazir found more similarities. Benazir and her siblings were raised as Sunni Muslims, like her father. The differences were never a problem for her family.

At home, Benazir spoke Sindhi, Persian, or English with her parents. She often spoke in a mixture of all three languages. She also had tutors for Urdu, the national language of Pakistan, and for Arabic, the language of Islam.

Reading the Koran, the holy book of Islam, in Arabic is a duty for Muslims, and Benazir studied Arabic so that she could read the Koran in its original language. She believed the Koran was her most important subject, but Arabic was a difficult language for her to learn. Benazir and her sister, Sanam, learned from reading the Koran that:

Muslim history was full of women who had taken a public role and performed every bit as successfully as men. Nothing in Islam discouraged them, or me [Benazir], from pursuing that course.

Much of the religious training Benazir received came from her mother. She grew up watching her mother pray five times a day, no matter where she was in the world. When Benazir was 9, her mother began teaching her how to pray. First, they washed

Praying Muslims face Mecca, birthplace of the prophet Muhammad, the founder of Islam.

their hands, feet, and faces. Then, facing the holy city of Mecca in Saudi Arabia, mother and daughter bent down in prayer to Allah, the Muslim name for God.

Benazir's father had entered politics when she was just 4, and for much of her childhood, she saw him in the newspaper more than in person. She and her siblings lived with servants at the house in Karachi, or they lived at boarding schools. Benazir's father promised that if the children studied hard, he would send all of them to the United States for college.

Benazir did well at her studies. At the convent school in Karachi, and later at a boarding school in Murree, in the foothills of the Himalayas, Benazir loved to study and learn. Benazir was the eldest child, and that made her feel an extra responsibility. It was important for her to set a good example for her siblings and to make her father proud. She wrote:

> *My father put a great emphasis on education, and I found that he would always be so pleased when I did well. ... I had a love for learning.*

Though Benazir heard about politics from her father, she and her sister, Sanam, did not worry much about the world outside of school. After class, they played jacks with goat bones and read books. But in September 1965, India and Pakistan went to war over control of Kashmir province. The road from India to

Kashmir ran right through Murree.

The Catholic nuns at the boarding school prepared their students for a possible attack by the Indian army. They taught the girls to get up at night and run quickly to an air-raid shelter in case of attack. Benazir took responsibility for her sister, who was also a student at the school. She tied Sanam's slippers to her feet at night so that in an emergency they wouldn't waste time looking for slippers.

For 12-year-old Benazir and 9-year-old Sanam, the preparations for war were exciting. They played a game with their classmates in which they gave each other false names in case they were kidnapped. Most of the boarding school's students were the daughters of Pakistani politicians, and the girls were told that they might be used as hostages if they were captured by enemy troops. The danger was real, but it did not seem real to them. India and Pakistan fought in Kashmir for 17 days, but the fighting never reached Benazir's school.

Kashmir province is located in the mountains north of Pakistan. The British government divided Kashmir between India and Pakistan in 1947. Though most of the people in Kashmir were Muslims, India claimed the eastern two-thirds of Kashmir, and Pakistan was given the western third. The two countries both believe they should rule Kashmir, and the province has caused many problems between them. India and Pakistan went to war over Kashmir in 1947–1948, and again in 1965, when Benazir was at Murree. In 2002, both countries threatened to use nuclear weapons if they went to war.

3 A GROWING AWARENESS

❧⟨✕⟩☙

When the war broke out over Kashmir, Zulfikar Bhutto was the foreign minister of Pakistan's government. He flew to the United Nations in New York City to present a plan for the people of Kashmir to decide on their own government. His plan was rejected. Instead, on September 23, 1965, the United Nations called for a cease-fire in Kashmir. The president of Pakistan, Ayub Khan, signed a peace treaty with India. Both countries agreed to pull their troops back to their original borders.

Many Pakistanis were angry that the government signed a peace treaty with India. They rioted in the streets and demanded that President Ayub Khan resign. Benazir's father was angry as well. He knew the treaty would not solve the problem of

Zulfikar Bhutto spoke to the U.N. General Assembly about a plan for Kashmiri self-government.

The conflict between Pakistan and India prompted many women to seek military training.

Kashmir, and he resigned from his position in Ayub Khan's government.

In 1967, Zulfikar started a new political party called the Pakistan People's Party (PPP). He spoke to large groups of Pakistanis all over the country. He encouraged them to "[c]all for democracy, where the vote of the poorest carries the same weight as the vote of the richest."

Fourteen-year-old Benazir began to take an interest in politics for the first time. She had heard her parents talk about politics for years, but they had sheltered her from many of the issues that troubled Pakistan. She went to the best schools and lived in nice houses. Her family had plenty of food to eat. She wore beautiful clothes—often new outfits that her father bought for her in New York City. But in the streets of Karachi, she later wrote, "I had seen people without shoes, without shirts, young girls with matted hair and thin babies." Benazir began to care about the problems of the poor people of Pakistan. She wondered, "Did the poor not even count as people?"

The Bhutto house in Karachi became the new PPP headquarters. Benazir and Sanam joined the PPP and helped their parents sign up

In an interview she gave in 2000, Benazir Bhutto recalled:

It was a very privileged life that we led with huge homes and scores of staff with everything looked after. ... Now the world has changed. ... There's a greater appreciation of each human being being equal and entitled to the same opportunity. ... In those days there was much less dignity. I remember that the poorer people would greet the richer people by bending down and touching their feet, or ... throwing themselves on their feet.

Zulfikar Bhutto rallied supporters at the founding of the Pakistan People's Party.

new members. At first, her father gave speeches in small rural towns to a few hundred people. Soon, her father was speaking to huge city crowds with thousands of people. President Khan had ruled Pakistan as a dictator for 11 years, and he saw Zulfikar Bhutto as a threat. The president did not want the people to vote for a new leader. He also believed that Benazir's father promoted rioting by university students and the poor.

In 1968, President Khan arrested Benazir's father

and the leaders of the PPP and put them in prison. The president then closed all schools and universities to try to stop the riots. Benazir had finished her classes but could not go to school to study for her final high school exams. While Benazir's mother and siblings moved to be near Zulfikar's prison in Lahore, Benazir stayed in Karachi with the servants. Her father hired tutors to help her study. In addition to her final high school exams, he wanted her to take the American SAT college entrance exam so that she could attend college in the United States. Every day, Benazir studied her subjects with her tutors. At night, she sometimes joined her friends for a swim at a country club near her home. She enjoyed spending time with her friends, but she worried constantly about her father, and she missed her family.

In December 1968, Benazir took her exams in secret because Pakistan's schools were still closed. The Catholic nuns from her school arranged for her to take her finals and the SAT at the Vatican Embassy. Her father wrote her a letter from prison to congratulate her. She was only 15, three years younger than he was when he took his exams. He wrote, "At this rate, you might become the president."

While Benazir was preparing for and taking her exams, people all over Pakistan were demanding that Benazir's father be released from prison. Benazir's mother, Nusrat, led protest marches in Lahore.

Pakistani citizens protested the imprisonment of Zulfikar Bhutto.

President Khan used the Pakistani army to try to stop the riots. The army broke up many protests with tear gas. Nusrat carried a wet towel in a plastic bag to use if the police or army fired tear gas. She placed the wet towel over her nose to protect her lungs from the stinging, choking gas. Finally, in an effort to stop the riots, President Khan agreed to release Zulfikar Bhutto and the other PPP leaders.

Soon after her father's release, Benazir and her sister rode with their parents in a victory parade near Al-Murtaza. A huge crowd celebrated around their open car. Suddenly, Zulfikar ordered the girls to duck. A man in the crowd tried to shoot him, but the gun jammed. The crowd took away the man's gun and beat him nearly to death. Benazir's father called for the crowd to let the man go and show mercy. The crowd released the man, but Benazir never forgot her fear for her father's life.

Benazir was learning to take such violence for granted. She later wrote, "This was the life of politics in Pakistan, and therefore the life we led. Death threats. Corruption. Violence." When her father began to campaign again for a new government, Benazir learned about the many problems facing Pakistan. The majority of Pakistan's people were very poor and uneducated. Most could not read or write. Benazir realized that when people were frustrated and wanted change in the government, it often led to violence.

After her father was released from prison, he began a hunger strike to protest against President Khan's government. For months, Zulfikar did not eat. People all over Pakistan joined him in his protest. When President Khan realized that he could not stop people from starving themselves to death, he resigned. Instead of allowing democratic elections to decide the country's next leader, however, he turned the government over to the army. President Yahya Khan, the new leader, immediately declared martial law and sent the army to stop the protests. ✍

4 TO COLLEGE AND BACK

Chapter

❧

When Benazir took the SAT entrance exams for college in the United States, she did so with the hope that she would follow in her father's footsteps and study at the University of California at Berkeley. Her father, however, had different ideas. He chose Radcliffe College for her, which was a part of Harvard University. Radcliffe College was in Cambridge, Massachusetts, and Zulfikar thought the cold Massachusetts weather would force Benazir to study more. In April 1969, she received an acceptance letter from Radcliffe. She was only 16 years old and very shy, but she was excited to leave Pakistan for the school year.

That August, Benazir's father gave her a beautiful Koran as a going-away present. Benazir stood in the

On a trip with her father, Benazir Bhutto met with a member of India's government.

doorway of her house in Karachi. Her mother passed the new Koran over her head, and Benazir kissed it. As she and her mother drove to the airport, Benazir became the first woman in the Bhutto family to go overseas to college.

Benazir's mother stayed with her for the first three weeks of school. She helped Benazir move into her dormitory and showed her the direction of Mecca so she could say her prayers. Nusrat also had special Pakistani clothing made for Benazir. Most of the traditional shalwar kamiz in Pakistan were made of cotton or silk, but Nusrat had new shalwar kamiz made of wool to keep Benazir warm during Boston's cold winters.

Benazir felt like a stranger in this new country. Most of the students she met did not know where Pakistan was, and Benazir had to explain to them that it was near India. She stood out in her traditional clothing, and this made her feel uncomfortable. Soon after her mother left for home, Benazir went to the school store and bought jeans and sweatshirts. Her Islamic traditions required her to cover herself in public, but she figured that jeans and sweatshirts covered her as well as shalwar kamiz. In jeans, she blended in with the rest of the Radcliffe students and felt like less of a stranger.

Benazir adapted to the United States quickly. She made friends with the other girls in her dormitory.

They studied together, went to movies, and walked to a nearby ice cream shop. She learned to love peppermint ice cream, a flavor she had not known in Pakistan. She had always studied hard, and she

Women in Kashmir province wear traditional shalwar kamiz.

continued to do well in college. As she got over her shyness, she wrote for the college newspaper and led tours for new students.

When Benazir first arrived at Radcliffe, she had planned to study psychology. She soon discovered

Benazir came to love her experience in the United States at Harvard's Radcliffe College in snowy New England

that many psychology courses required students to dissect animals. She loved the many family dogs and cats she had grown up with at home and did not want to cut up animals. She decided instead to study comparative government. In her classes, she studied different forms of government, such as dictatorship,

communism, and democracy. Benazir found that she already knew more about government than many of her classmates. For example, she understood that a dictator, like President Khan, could arrest her father just for speaking out against the Pakistani government.

Pakistan seemed very far away, but Benazir's parents wrote often and sent her Pakistani newspapers. She listened to news reports and radio broadcasts from England to get news about her home country. In December 1970, President Yahya Khan allowed democratic elections. Benazir stayed up all night to hear the results. Early in the morning, her mother called to say that her father and the PPP had won more than half the seats in the National Assembly. Benazir was proud of her father, but she felt sad that she was not in Pakistan to celebrate with her family.

Zulfikar Bhutto contacted the other elected leaders to put together a government that would take over from President Yahya Khan. This government would write a new constitution that gave equal rights to all Pakistanis. But the elected leaders in East Pakistan did not want to join Bhutto and West

In the 1970 elections, the PPP won more than half the seats in the National Assembly in West Pakistan. But the Awami League of East Pakistan won many more seats than the PPP. Zulfikar and his party's refusal to accept this electoral defeat led to the breakup of the country in 1971.

Pakistan. They were upset that the recent election, which should have put East Pakistan leaders in charge of the National Assembly, had been "stolen" by Bhutto and the PPP. They wanted to declare East Pakistan independent. War broke out between East and West Pakistan early in 1971, and India soon lent East Pakistan its support.

The Indian army was too strong for West Pakistan. In December 1971, Zulfikar Bhutto went to the United Nations to ask the Security Council to order India to leave East Pakistan. Benazir joined her father at the United Nations. For four days, she sat behind her father and listened to him argue that Pakistan must remain one country. Benazir trusted her father, and she trusted the United Nations. She believed the Security Council would order India to withdraw from East Pakistan.

The United Nations, however, ruled against West Pakistan, and East Pakistan declared itself independent soon after. The new country was named Bangladesh. The politics of Pakistan were difficult for Benazir to understand. She believed, as her father did, that it was wrong to divide Pakistan. She believed that Islam held the two parts of her country together, no matter their differences. But things had changed, whether she liked it or not, and shortly after the war, her father became the new president of a much smaller Pakistan.

While her father was president, Benazir traveled many places with him during school vacations. In 1972, she met Indira Gandhi, the prime minister of India. Benazir was impressed with how well this strong woman ruled the huge country of India. No college course taught Benazir as much about government as these travels with her father.

In 1973, Benazir graduated from Radcliffe with a bachelor's degree in comparative government. She wanted to stay in the United States for graduate school, but her father had already enrolled her at Oxford University in England. He explained his

Benazir's father met with Indian Prime Minister Indira Gandhi (center) in 1972.

> *Benazir's time at Radcliffe had a profound influence on her. The women's movement had just begun, and students and citizens were actively protesting the Vietnam War. Benazir said that she found that "if you didn't like something you could do something about it."*

reasoning in a letter: "Four years in one place is more than enough. If you stay longer in America, you will begin to put down roots." For the first time in her life, Benazir tried to argue with her father. In the end, she followed her father's instructions and went to England.

In the fall of 1973, Benazir's father wrote her a letter to tell her how proud he was that she was at Oxford. He told her, "We pray and hope this dream turned into reality will grow into a magnificent career in the service of your people." From a young age, Benazir understood that her father wanted her to choose a career in government. She thought about a career in the foreign service. She was eager to travel and promote Pakistan to other countries, but she did not want to become a politician.

The four years she spent at Oxford were happy ones for Benazir. She drove around town in a yellow sports car, a graduation present from her father. Her friends knew her car and left messages for her on the windshield. She drove to London and went to plays. She ate plenty of peppermint ice cream, her favorite American flavor. She became very outgoing and joined the debate club to improve her speaking skills.

For the first three years at Oxford, Benazir studied politics, philosophy, and economics. In her fourth year, she took a special yearlong course in international law and diplomacy. She hoped this would prepare her for a position in Pakistan's foreign service.

On June 21, 1977, Benazir's 24th birthday, she gave a graduation party for her friends in the gardens near her dormitory. But it was also her going-away party. As she ate strawberries and cream and shared stories from her time at Oxford, Benazir collected her friends' home addresses. She looked forward to

Benazir was proud to attend Oxford University, where her father had also been a student.

returning to Pakistan after eight years of college.

The troubles in Pakistan had continued while Benazir was overseas. Though her father became prime minister in August 1973, violent riots and many arrests occurred before and after his election. At one point, the police from London's Scotland Yard visited Benazir at Oxford with a warning for her to be careful. They were concerned that enemies of her father might hurt her. She was careful, but the troubles in Pakistan seemed very far from England.

In June 1977, Benazir and her siblings all flew home for a family reunion. Her parents were living at the prime minister's home in Rawalpindi. It was only a few minutes from the government buildings in Islamabad, now the capital of Pakistan. The family enjoyed their time together in the gardens surrounding the huge house. Her father welcomed her home and told her he had found a job for her in the government. She immediately started her first job, sorting and organizing paperwork for her father.

When Pakistan became independent in 1947, Karachi was the capital. But because of its location, Karachi did not have room to grow as a capital city. President Ayub Khan proposed that a brand new capital city be built in the center of Pakistan. Islamabad was built on a plain near Rawalpindi. The city planners built sections for the government, the embassies, education, and business. Each section has wide avenues and large trees. People began moving to Islamabad in 1962, and the government finished the move in the 1980s.

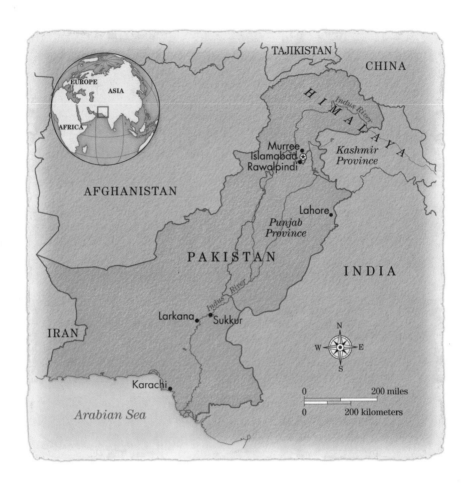

Only 10 days later, Benazir's life changed forever. Early in the morning on July 5, 1977, the Pakistani army, led by General Zia ul-Haq, forcibly took over the government of Pakistan. A friend warned Benazir's father that the army had surrounded him. Benazir's brothers wanted to defend themselves against the army, but Zulfikar told them, "Never resist a military coup [government takeover]. The generals want us

Islamabad became the capital of Pakistan after East Pakistan broke away to become Bangladesh.

dead." Zulfikar ordered his family to pack. He wanted them to fly to Karachi on the first plane. He did not want his family to be arrested or hurt. He knew the army really only wanted him.

The family waited all night for the army to arrest Zulfikar. Benazir's brothers got on the first plane to Karachi. Benazir's mother worried that the sons of a prime minister might be in more danger than his daughters would be. The three women, however, continued to wait for the army. At 8 A.M., Nusrat called to her daughters, "Pinkie! Sunny! Come quickly. Papa is leaving." Benazir ran down the steps and out the front door. Her father was in the back seat of his car. Benazir waved goodbye. Her father turned back to look at them, and the car drove away.

Benazir's father was taken to the family's summer home in Murree. He was placed under house arrest. He could not leave the house, and he could only use the telephone to call his family.

General Zia hoped that the Pakistani people would forget their popular leader if they did not hear from him. But in Karachi, Benazir and her mother spoke to huge crowds of people. General Zia

General Muhammad Zia ul-Haq (1924–1988) entered military service to the British army in 1943 and fought for the Allies in World War II. He later received military training in the United States. In 1976, he was appointed Pakistan's chief of army staff. He overthrew the administration that had appointed him just one year later.

decided that holding Zulfikar under arrest made him more popular, and so at the end of July, Zulfikar was released. The crowds that met him at the train station in Karachi were so large that it took 10 hours to drive the short distance to his house. ✺

The Bhuttos' summer home and young Benazir's convent school were located in the resort city of Murree.

5 THE PRISON YEARS

When General Zia took over the government in July, he promised that new elections would be held in October. Benazir's father planned to run for office again. But in September, soldiers again arrested Zulfikar. He was charged with planning a murder and taken to prison. For the next year, Benazir and her mother worked to get her father released. They were put under house arrest several times. Benazir's brothers again fled the country.

In March 1978, Benazir's father was convicted of his crime and received a death sentence. Benazir was alone in Karachi when she heard the news. Her mother was under house arrest near her father's prison in Rawalpindi, and her brothers and sister were out of the country. Benazir did not know who

Both Benazir and her mother, Nusrat, spent time imprisoned in Karachi Central Jail.

could help her, but she hoped that something could be done. The leaders of Russia, China, Turkey, Saudi Arabia, Canada, and Egypt had all asked General Zia to change her father's death sentence to life in prison.

Benazir worked with lawyers to file an appeal to Pakistan's Supreme Court. While waiting for the court's decision in March 1979, Benazir brought a secret visitor to her father's prison cell. She hid the family's small white dog, Happy, under her coat. A kind guard allowed her to bring the dog inside, and Happy sniffed his way along the prison hallway, searching for his master. When he found Zulfikar, Happy barked and jumped against the cell bars. Benazir wrote in her autobiography:

> *At least I could give my father that one moment, a reminder of life when we were a normal family … living under one roof, with dogs and cats in the garden.*

Late in March, the Supreme Court recommended that Zulfikar Bhutto have his sentence changed to life in prison. This was good news, but Benazir knew that General Zia would make the final decision. She and her mother had again been placed under house arrest—this time in a police camp near Rawalpindi. She paced the floor of their tiny room, hoping that somehow her father's life would be spared. Pope John Paul II, as well as leaders from England, Russia,

Both Benazir's brothers (in turtleneck and sports coat) protested their father's sentence in London, England.

Saudi Arabia, and the United States, asked General Zia to show mercy.

On the morning of April 3, 1979, Benazir and her mother were taken to see her father. Usually, they visited him on different days, and both of them knew what this meant. Benazir's father sat on the floor of his cell, surprised to see both of them. He asked his guard if this was the last meeting with his family. The guard nodded. Benazir and her mother were not allowed to enter his cell. They had to touch his hands through the bars.

Zulfikar told them how proud he was of his

family. He gave them permission to leave Pakistan if they wanted a different life. Both Benazir and her mother told him they would not leave. They did not want the generals to think they had given up the fight for democracy. Benazir's father turned to her and said, "You don't know how much I love you, how much I've always loved you. You are my jewel."

Early the next morning, Zulfikar Bhutto was hanged. After he was dead, the army quietly took his body to the family graveyard near Al-Murtaza. They buried him secretly so that his supporters would not know that it had happened. Benazir and her mother were told the next morning. They were not allowed to accompany his body to the graveyard, a family duty for Muslims.

Zulfikar Ali Bhutto (1928–1979)

Less than two years after her return to Pakistan, Benazir's life had become a nightmare of violent arrests, family separations, and prison cells. With her father gone, she did not know what to do next. In her last meeting with him, she had promised him she would carry on his fight for democracy. The death of her father changed Benazir's life. She decided then that she would follow her father's path and work to bring justice and respect for human rights back to Pakistan.

Three days after her father was buried in April 1979, Benazir and her mother received permission to visit his grave. Army officers took them to the family graveyard near Al-Murtaza. Her father's grave was unmarked. Only a mound of fresh dirt covered with rose petals showed Benazir where her father lay buried. As she knelt at the foot of the grave, Benazir remembered something her father told her when she was about to leave for college. He took her to the same graveyard and said:

> *You are going far away to America ... but remember, whatever happens to you, you will ultimately return here. Your place is here. Your roots are here. ... It is here that you will be buried.*

Benazir felt so sad at the loss of her father that she could not eat or drink. She dreamed that her father was not really dead. Her mother brought her soup and forced her to

In her last meeting with her father, Zulfikar gave Benazir permission to leave Pakistan and live somewhere where she would be free. But Benazir chose to remain in Pakistan. She told him, "No, papa, I will continue the struggle that you began for democracy."

eat. A few weeks after her father's death, she and her mother were released from house arrest, and they returned to Karachi.

Less than six months after their release, General Zia arrested them again and placed them under house arrest at Al-Murtaza. Under house arrest, Benazir and her mother were not allowed to leave the house or gardens for any reason. Their phone service was cut,

General Zia ul-Haq came to power in a military overthrow in 1977.

and only Benazir's sister, Sanam, could visit them. Many times, the electricity was cut off as well. Armed soldiers surrounded the house to keep them in and to keep visitors out. Nusrat played cards to pass the time. Benazir tried to keep the flowers alive in the garden.

In March 1980, Benazir and her mother were abruptly freed. They returned to their house in Karachi, but they feared they would be arrested again. They planned their travels and appearances so that they were never together. They hoped this would prevent General Zia from arresting both of them at the same time.

On March 13, 1981, Benazir and her mother were arrested once again, but this time they were separated. They put Nusrat in Karachi Central Jail. Benazir was sent to a prison in the desert city of Sukkur. Benazir was not told why she was arrested, and she did not know where her mother had been sent.

That night, a group known as Al-Zulfikar hijacked a Pakistan International Airline plane. Al-Zulfikar planned to throw General Zia out of office and return democracy to Pakistan. The hijackers demanded the release of Pakistani political prisoners. General Zia arrested thousands of Pakistanis he believed knew about this group. When her guards showed her a newspaper, Benazir learned for the first time about the hijacking. Worse, she read

Al-Zulfikar's goal was to overthrow the military regime that ousted Zulfikar Bhutto. Al-Zulfikar was funded by the security agencies of both Afghanistan and India, both of whom were opposed to the Zia regime. The 1981 hijacking was rumored to be linked to the assassination of Zahoorul Hasan Bhopali, a Zia aide.

that her brothers were part of Al-Zulfikar. Benazir and her mother had not heard from her brothers since they left Pakistan in 1977, but General Zia believed they were helping the brothers.

Benazir had only the clothes she had been wearing when she was arrested. Her prison cell had barred windows on all four walls. She felt like she was living in a cage. She had no sweaters, socks, or blankets, and the desert nights were cold. She tried to sleep on her rope cot, but she was so cold her teeth chattered. She was kept in solitary confinement and was not allowed to receive any visitors. The only people she saw were the guards who brought her weak tea, bread, and watery soup twice a day. Occasionally, she got fish. Benazir began to lose weight and felt sick most of the time.

Benazir spent five months in the prison at Sukkur. She had frequent earaches and skin rashes, and her hair began to fall out. She thought of her father's brave smile in prison, and decided she had to stay alive. Her mother sent her letters from her jail cell in Karachi. Nusrat told her to eat lots of fruit and vegetables. Benazir got few vegetables, and she never got fruit, but she began to eat the food the guards brought to her.

Benazir was given one newspaper a day, and she read every word. Most of the news was about the hijacking, but she read every story, even the puzzles for children. She tried to exercise by running in place. She walked around the empty courtyard if the guards opened her cell. A kind guard brought her a small notebook, and she tried to write for an hour every day.

When summer came, it got extremely hot in Sukkur. Temperatures rose to 120 degrees Fahrenheit (49 degrees Celsius) some days. Benazir dreamed of cool, clean water and peppermint ice cream. She imagined she was eating steak and mushrooms with her school friends in Oxford. In a letter, Nusrat told Benazir that she poured water over her head several times a day. She said that while her clothes dried, she didn't feel as hot. Benazir tried it, and she felt comfortable for the short time it took for her clothes to dry.

Whenever Benazir felt afraid, she prayed. Many people in Pakistan had suffered more than she did. She heard rumors that many of the PPP

While in prison, Benazir found strength in her religious beliefs. Denied comfort and companionship, she spent much of her time in prayer and realized that her relationship with God was the only thing her jailers could not take from her. Instead of losing faith, imprisonment strengthened her beliefs.

leaders had been beaten and tortured in prison. She prayed for their release from prison. She also prayed for her mother's release—and her own. In June 1981, Benazir wrote in a small notebook:

> *I have coped. Each moment has dragged, but it has also passed. God alone has helped me in this ordeal. Without him, I would have perished [died].*

On June 21, 1981, Benazir turned 28 years old. Her sister, Sanam, came to visit her in jail. Sanam cried when she saw how thin and sick Benazir looked. During the hour-long visit, Benazir asked Sanam to tell her about their friends and family. Sanam told her she might marry, but she wanted to wait until Benazir and their mother got out of jail. Benazir told Sanam to go ahead and plan the wedding. She would feel better if Sanam had a husband to protect her.

Sanam was married in September at the family home in Karachi. Benazir was surprised when she was allowed to attend Sanam's wedding. For two days, Benazir did not sleep. She took long hot baths. She talked to her mother, who had been released for health reasons in July. She talked to the many relatives who came for the wedding. The guests danced and sang for days. The music and voices filled Benazir's ears. After six months alone, Benazir felt joy at the music and singing, surrounded by her

family and friends. In the three years she was under arrest, it was the only time Benazir left her cell.

On the morning of the third day, the police came for Benazir. She had prepared for her return to jail by packing her bag with extra clothes, magazines, and newspapers. The police took her to Karachi Central Jail where she was placed in her mother's old cell. Three days after her return to jail, Benazir received news that her sentence had been extended another three months. Unless she agreed to stay out of politics, General Zia would not release her from jail. ॐ

Armed guards patrolled the jails where Benazir and her mother were imprisoned.

Chapter

6 LIVING IN EXILE

∾

In December 1981, Benazir Bhutto was moved from the Karachi Central Jail to Al-Murtaza, her family's summer home, where she was again kept under house arrest. Only her mother, sister, and an aunt were allowed to visit. Karachi was an hour away by plane, and her relatives could not come often. Bhutto's mother, too, was ill and unable to visit.

Nusrat had become very sick while she was in jail. She lost weight and began coughing up blood. She had been released from jail in July 1981, but she was kept under house arrest in Karachi. Her doctors believed she had lung cancer, and they asked for permission for her to go to Europe for better treatment. The government refused.

In November 1982, Nusrat finally received

The crescent moon on the top of a tower in London's Whitechapel district is a symbol of Islam. The city is home to a sizable Muslim population.

permission to travel to Europe. Benazir was taken to see her mother before she left for Germany. Nusrat was in bed and needed a wheelchair to move around. Bhutto wanted her mother to get well, but she was afraid to be alone in Pakistan.

When her mother left Pakistan, Sanam went with her. Only Bhutto stayed behind. She was now under house arrest in Karachi. She worried about her mother, and she missed her family. She began to have more earaches, a problem she'd had off and on in prison. Her ear became seriously infected, and she needed surgery. Her doctor asked for permission for her to leave Pakistan, but the government did not answer.

Finally, on January 10, 1984, Bhutto received permission to fly to London for treatment. She traveled first to Switzerland, where her mother met her at the airport. Even when she saw her mother, looking well after her treatment, Bhutto could not believe she was free. She had been inside either a house or a prison cell for three years. She stared at the mountains and breathed the fresh air.

When she went to her mother's apartment, both of her brothers called to talk to her. She had not heard their voices for more than seven years. Her brother Mir brought his Afghan wife and their young daughter, Fathi, to visit. Her other brother, Shah Nawaz, lived in France, so he could not get there before she left for London. They promised to meet after her surgery.

When Bhutto arrived in London with her sister Sanam, a huge crowd of Pakistanis met her at the airport. London police were called in to control the crowd. Bhutto felt like she was back in Pakistan during a happier time. The people called her name and her father's name as she moved through the crowd. News reporters asked her if she had gone into exile and left Pakistan for good. She answered, "I was

Bhutto had become familiar with London during her time as a student in Oxford, England.

born in Pakistan and I'm going to die in Pakistan. My grandfather is buried there. My father is buried there. I will never leave my country."

By the time Bhutto had her surgery, she was almost deaf in her left ear. She had also lost feeling on the left side of her face. The surgery was successful, but it took weeks for Bhutto to recover. She had to lie flat on her back, unable to sit up without becoming dizzy. Bhutto planned to return to Pakistan as soon as she was well. Her mother and sister begged her to stay in Europe. They feared General Zia would put her back in prison if she returned.

In London, Bhutto could move around freely. Still, she was afraid to leave her aunt's apartment. She feared that General Zia had sent men to follow her. The traffic and city noise bothered her, and she felt uncomfortable in crowds. Bhutto had become quite famous in London for standing up to General Zia, and many people recognized her in the street. For the more than 350,000 Pakistanis living in exile in England in 1984, she was a national hero. She found the courage to hold her head high, despite her many fears.

Bhutto thought about how she could continue the fight against General Zia's government from England. She had many friends in Pakistan who sent her letters about prisoners held for years under Zia's martial law. General Zia controlled the newspapers in Pakistan, so much of the world did not know about his human rights abuses. Bhutto began to write letters to English and American newspapers about Pakistan's political prisoners. Amnesty International, an organization that defended human rights around the world, helped Bhutto get the word out.

Bhutto rented an apartment in London, and it became the headquarters for the PPP in England. Young Pakistani exiles helped answer the phone and type letters. Bhutto began to write letters to the United Nations, the U.S. secretary of state for human rights, and to members of the British Parliament. She

In 2001, Amnesty International celebrated its 40-year anniversary with a candle festival. The candle is the organization's symbol of hope.

Founded in 1961 by British lawyer Peter Benenson, Amnesty International now has members in 150 countries. The organization believes that all people are born free and equal. It supports the rights of all people to be free from torture, slavery, and illegal arrest. Amnesty International raises money from memberships and donations. It does not accept money from governments.

included photographs of Pakistani political prisoners and summarized their stories of illegal arrest and torture.

When Bhutto heard of a prisoner being sentenced to death, she and her volunteers worked all night to get the letters out quickly. She worked hard to bring the truth about the military trials and executions to the world's attention. In some cases, Bhutto's letters received attention in the newspapers and from world governments. In others, the prisoners were executed even though Amnesty International and world leaders protested. General Zia denied that the prisoners' letters were true, and the military trials continued.

By the fall of 1984, the United States began to pressure General Zia to allow democratic elections. He announced that he would allow elections in February 1985. Bhutto wanted to return home for the elections, but she was told she would be arrested if she returned. Though General Zia agreed to elections, he passed new laws for political candidates. The candidates could not hold outdoor meetings or speak on television or radio. Just before the election,

General Zia arrested 3,000 political leaders who opposed his government.

Pakistani women voted at a polling station in the village of Attock.

Despite the election results, which strongly favored the PPP, General Zia amended the constitution to allow him to continue in power. Bhutto saw that nothing had changed in Pakistan. She continued to fight from England for the lives of Pakistan's political prisoners. She spoke to the Council on Foreign Relations in New York City and the European Parliament in Strasbourg, France. She reminded the governments of the United States and Europe that they continued to send financial assistance to the government of Pakistan even though they knew of the human rights abuses there.

In July 1985, Bhutto flew to southern France for a family reunion at her brother Shah's home in Cannes. Her mother, sister, brothers, and their families planned to have a barbecue on the beach. Mir and Shah had married Afghan sisters when they lived in Afghanistan, and Bhutto hoped to get to know her sisters-in-law better.

The afternoon picnic of barbecued chicken and Pakistani dishes reminded Bhutto of family picnics on the beach in Karachi when they were children. She chased her nieces along the beach and laughed and teased her brothers. When her father died and the family scattered, Bhutto never thought they would be together again. For one day on the beach in France, far from home, her family came together and enjoyed their freedom.

The happy times did not last long. That night, after the family left the beach, Shah was poisoned and died. His wife called the family, who called an ambulance and then rushed to Shah's house. Bhutto begged the ambulance drivers to take him to the hospital, but Shah had been dead for several hours when his wife called them. The police investigated Shah's death as a murder, but they were unable to determine who had given him the poison.

Following Islamic law, the family had a holy man wash Shah's body and dress him in a simple burial

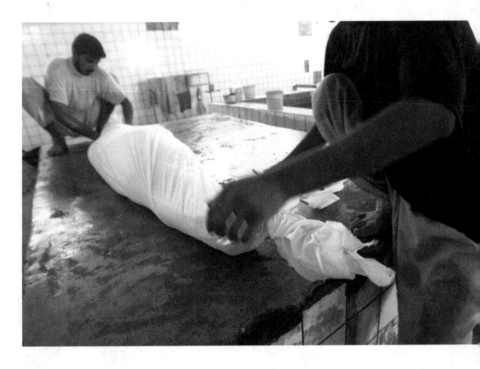

After death, the dead are washed and wrapped, according to Islamic law.

shroud. Bhutto and Sanam took his body home to be buried at Al-Murtaza. General Zia blocked the roads. He did not want a huge crowd gathering to greet the Bhuttos. But when their plane approached the airport, Bhutto saw thousands of people lining the roads leading to the airport.

Shah was buried near his father in the family graveyard. In her sadness, Bhutto remembered her father teaching her about loyalty to Pakistan. She wrote, "As children we had been taught that no price was too high to pay for our country. But the personal price to our family had been high."

7 RETURN TO PAKISTAN

❧

In April 1986, Bhutto returned to Pakistan—this time to stay. As her plane circled the airport in Lahore, the pilot announced, "We welcome Miss Benazir Bhutto back to Pakistan." Bhutto stared out her window as the plane banked. Below her, she saw the bright green fields of Punjab province, but she could not see the airport. The pilot told her that more than a million people were waiting for her outside the airport gates.

Bhutto had planned for her return for several months. Friends warned her that she might be arrested again—or even killed. But she wanted to go home. She took foreign reporters with her in hopes that they would protect her from General Zia. The general would not want the reporters to write stories

Bhutto spent time with her ailing mother on her wedding day, December 18, 1987.

about him in foreign newspapers.

Her Pakistani friends met her at the terminal and led her to a brightly painted truck. She climbed up on the truck to ride to a nearby park to speak. Bhutto had never seen such a crowd, not even with her father. In her autobiography, she wrote:

> *There are moments in life which are not possible to describe. My return to Lahore was one of them. The sea of humanity lining the roads, jammed on balconies and roofs, wedged in trees and on lampposts, walking alongside the truck ... was more like an ocean.*

It took more than 10 hours to drive the short distance to the park. The crowd grew along the way. Millions of Pakistanis came to hear Bhutto speak that day.

Bhutto continued to tour Pakistan, and she spoke to crowds at every stop. People lined the roads between the cities. Though she was arrested and placed in jail for three weeks that August, Bhutto immediately returned to her work at her home in Karachi. She met with the leaders of all the political parties that opposed General Zia. She called for democratic elections and asked her supporters to work peacefully. She did not want any violence.

Bhutto was 32 years old when she returned to

Benazir Bhutto spoke to a crowd as leader of the Pakistan People's Party.

Pakistan. Already she had lived a very unusual life. Most Pakistani women her age had been married for many years. During her college years, her mother and aunts had looked for a suitable husband for her, but Bhutto thought she would meet someone and marry for love. After her father's death and her years in prison, however, Bhutto began to listen to her mother. She agreed to think about an arranged marriage.

Benazir Bhutto was very famous in Pakistan. Many Pakistanis thought of her as their sister or daughter. She did not have the privacy to go on dates and get to know possible husbands. She worked long hours on party business. She had dedicated her life to bringing

Bhutto greeted crowds in the street as she campaigned for the PPP.

freedom back to Pakistan, and she needed a husband who understood the importance of her career. But she did not think any Pakistani man would agree to marry a woman who wanted a career and a family.

In July 1987, Bhutto agreed to meet Asif Zardari, a man her aunt wanted her to consider for marriage.

Though she had met him once before, she did not remember anything about him. Zardari had even asked for her hand in marriage five years earlier, but it wasn't a good time for her. Now, Bhutto met with his mother and discussed her concerns. Zardari's mother told her he was a confident man who owned his own business. He understood that Bhutto was a politician, and he would support her in her work.

Bhutto met Zardari and his family in London. She did not want her private life to be news as it would be in Pakistan. For seven days, the two families met for dinner. Every morning, Zardari sent her roses and presents. But after four days, Bhutto still had not formed an opinion of him. Each morning when her mother asked if she had decided, Bhutto said she was not sure.

One day, Bhutto took her niece to the park. While she was there, she was stung by a bee. Her hand swelled badly from the bee sting. When Zardari arrived to take her out to dinner, he worried

Many Pakistani families arrange marriages for their sons and daughters. In arranged marriages, the mothers and aunts look for a good partner for the young adult. The parents look for good families with similar backgrounds and culture. In very traditional families, the bride and groom do not see each other until the wedding. After the ceremony, the bride goes to live with her husband's family. The husband decides who she sees, and if she goes out. Today, more families allow their children to find a marriage partner. Bhutto was the only sibling in her family to choose an arranged marriage.

that her hand might be infected. He took her to the doctor and made sure she had the right medication. For the first time, Bhutto saw that he was both kind and caring.

Seven days after she met Zardari, she told her mother she would marry him. Both families were thrilled. The wedding was set for December, and Bhutto returned to Pakistan. Zardari called her every night. He told her he remembered her when they were teenagers in Karachi. His father owned the theater where Bhutto went to the movies with her friends. Bhutto did not love Zardari, but she felt comfortable with him.

Bhutto was too busy to take time off for a traditional wedding. In Pakistan, the bride stays home for two weeks before the wedding. She sees no one but the family. The groom traditionally gives the bride 20 to 50 expensive outfits and seven sets of jewelry for the wedding. But Bhutto asked for just two outfits—one for the wedding and one for the reception—and only two sets of jewelry. She hoped their simple wedding would help change the wedding customs that sometimes left Pakistani families in debt for years.

Bhutto's mother returned to Karachi for the wedding. She had not been back to Pakistan for five years. Her brother Mir wanted to attend the wedding, but it was too dangerous. Bhutto wore a white dress

embroidered with gold thread. Her cousin asked her three times if she accepted Zardari. Each time she said yes. By tradition, she was now married.

Bhutto and her husband had both public and private wedding ceremonies.

After the family celebration, Zardari and Bhutto went to a public celebration at a stadium in Karachi. More than 200,000 people crowded into the stadium to wish them well. The people danced and cheered for the new couple. Bhutto had worried that her supporters might think she would leave politics now that she was married. But the crowd in the stadium proved the people of Pakistan had accepted her marriage. ✃

8 PRIME MINISTER BENAZIR BHUTTO

❦

In 1988, Pakistan experienced violence and protests in nearly every part of the country. General Zia appeared unable to control the ethnic and regional conflicts. In May, he dismissed the prime minister and dissolved the National Assembly. He blamed the violence on his political opponents. He announced that a general election would be held in the fall.

Bhutto did not believe the news. She was certain that General Zia would find a way to prevent the PPP from participating in the general election. Around the same time, Bhutto and Zardari announced that they were expecting a baby. Her family joked that General Zia announced elections because she would be unable to campaign. But Bhutto continued campaigning throughout Pakistan. Her pregnancy

When Benazir Bhutto became prime minister, she was only 35 years old, making her one of the youngest heads of state in the world.

hardly slowed her down.

In August, General Zia and most of his generals were killed in a plane crash. Investigators believed the plane had been blown up, but no one knew who had planned the murder of Zia. Pakistan was suddenly without a government. According to the constitution, the president of the Senate would form a temporary government until elections could be held. But everyone waited to see if the army would take over once again.

After General Zia's death, people displayed posters to commemorate his rule.

The temporary president, Ghulam Ishaq Khan, announced that elections would be held in November as planned. Bhutto now felt that her party might win the elections. If the people were allowed to vote, she felt sure the PPP would win a majority of seats in the National Assembly. She spent hours in meetings and traveled to every part of Pakistan. She promised Pakistanis basic human rights. She believed that all people deserved a decent home, a job, enough to eat, and an education. She also believed they deserved a fair trial if they were accused of a crime.

In late August, Bhutto felt sick and went to her doctor. There was trouble with her pregnancy, and the doctor told her she would have to slow down. He put her on bed rest for at least two hours every day.

In September, the doctor decided to deliver the baby surgically. Her son was born on September 21—five weeks early. He was small but healthy. Bhutto and

Pakistan's government is based on the British parliamentary system. Representatives are elected to the National Assembly and the Senate. The prime minister is usually the leader of the largest political party in the National Assembly. The president is the chief of state. Pakistan has returned to the parliamentary system each time democratic elections are held. But when the government is overthrown by the military, the army usually dismisses the government. Today, General Pervez Musharraf is the president. Pakistanis did not elect him as the president. Instead, he declared himself president in 2001.

Zardari named him Bilawal, which means "one without equal." Five days after her baby was born, Bhutto went back to work.

On November 16, Bhutto and her family returned to Al-Murtaza to vote. It was the first time she had ever voted in an election. The PPP won all of the seats in her home province of Sindh, as well as 92 of the 215 seats in the National Assembly. Though it was not a majority, it was more than any other party won, and it allowed the PPP to name the next prime minister. On December 1, 1988, Bhutto became the first woman prime minister of Pakistan.

Pakistani citizens rallied to support Bhutto in her new role as prime minister.

She had fought for democratic elections for 11 years. Pakistanis shouted her name in the streets as they celebrated.

But Bhutto had little time to celebrate. General Zia had left many problems. Millions of Pakistanis were unemployed. Prices for basic foods were too expensive for the poor. Flooding had caused many farmers to lose their crops. Pakistan owed huge amounts of money to other countries. Bhutto had thought that being elected was the hard part, but she soon realized that the real work was still ahead.

Bhutto ordered 1,000 political prisoners released her first day in office. She looked for money to pay for programs for the poor. She wanted to build health clinics and schools. But Pakistan was so far in debt that she spent the first year trying to find sources of money from other countries.

Pakistan continued to have problems with violence and terrorism. Bhutto had to send the army into Karachi to stop a riot. The religious leaders refused to support her government because she was a woman. More than 3 million refugees from Afghanistan were camped on Pakistan's northwest border. In the National Assembly, Bhutto and the PPP did not have enough votes to pass new laws.

But Bhutto did her best. She arrived at her office in Islamabad early every morning. After a full day of meetings, she often had late meetings with foreign ambassadors and politicians. In June 1989, U.S. President George H.W. Bush invited her to the White House. He promised her that the United States would help her. But he also asked her to tell him if Pakistan had nuclear weapons. The United States did not trade with countries that developed nuclear weapons, and many people believed Pakistan was building nuclear bombs.

Prime Minister Benazir Bhutto discussed Pakistan's nuclear capabilities with U.S. President George H.W. Bush.

Pakistan had started a nuclear weapons program when Bhutto's father was prime minister. The army kept the program very secret, and Bhutto did not

know for sure what Pakistan's capabilities were. From her point of view though, India was Pakistan's largest enemy. Many Pakistanis feared that India would attack them if they did not have the same weapons. And if India attacked Pakistan with nuclear weapons, they believed they needed the same kind of weapons to protect their country.

Bhutto's party also had many opponents in the National Assembly. The strongest party, the Pakistan Muslim League, wanted Pakistan to follow strict Islamic laws. The leader of the Muslim League, Nawaz Sharif, argued constantly with Bhutto about the future of Pakistan. Finally, in August 1990, the president dismissed Bhutto and the National Assembly. The president said that her government had not been able to bring law and order to Pakistan, and the economy was worse than when she took over. Sharif accused her government of corruption as well.

> *Pakistan and India had raced to develop a nuclear weapons program since India first tested a nuclear device in 1974. In May 1998, India conducted the first test of the country's newly developed nuclear weapons. Though world leaders asked Pakistan not to test weapons in retaliation, Prime Minister Nawaz Sharif declared that India "had radically altered the strategic balance in our region," and Pakistan needed its own nuclear weapons to restore the balance of power. Two weeks after India's tests, Pakistan proved its nuclear capabilities by conducting the first underground nuclear tests in the country's history.*

In the new elections, Nawaz Sharif and other Islamic parties won a majority of votes. Bhutto remained in the National Assembly as the leader of the opposition. Sharif, now prime minister, proposed a program to improve Pakistan's economy. He also cut most ties with the United States. This caused more trouble in the economy, and the violence in Pakistan became overwhelming. Terrorists bombed mosques and Christian churches. Illegal drugs came into Pakistan from Afghanistan, and many drug runners carried machine guns to defend the drugs.

By July 1993, the government was at a standstill. The politicians could not agree on a path to return law and order. The army told both the president and Prime Minister Sharif to resign for the good of the country. On July 18, both resigned, and a temporary prime minister tried to clean up the government before the next election.

Through all the chaos, Bhutto believed she could bring democracy to her country. In October 1993, she became prime minister once again. This time, she included opposition leaders in her government. She looked for compromise so that the government could work on Pakistan's problems, instead of fighting.

In her second term, Bhutto worked to improve education by building more schools. She made sure Pakistani children were vaccinated against polio. She made a plan to bring electricity to every house

As prime minister, Bhutto attended the opening of a new natural gas pipeline.

in small rural villages. She tried to stop the violence that spread across the country. But when Bhutto joined with Islamic leaders, she began to lose the support of Pakistanis who did not want religion in the government.

In addition to many problems she had faced before, Bhutto faced a new conflict with her family. Her brother, Mir, had returned to run in the elections in 1993. He did not join the PPP but instead started a party named after their father. Mir did not want to take over the PPP, but he claimed his new party was closer to the wishes of Zulfikar. With the help of their

Bhutto had a complicated relationship with her brother Mir Murtaza.

mother, he won his seat in the provincial elections.

In September 1996, Mir was shot and killed by policemen outside his house in Karachi. The gun battle took place late at night, and no one was sure if it was started by Mir and his men or if it was a murder. Bhutto had lost her last brother. Two months later, the president again dismissed her government. That night, the army arrested 20 people for the murder of Mir. To Bhutto's surprise, the army accused her husband of planning her brother's murder.

Zardari was arrested and put in jail to await trial. As Bhutto tried to defend her husband against the charges, Nawaz Sharif again accused her of corruption. She and Zardari were accused of stealing large amounts of money from the government. Many in Pakistan believe that Bhutto did not know about the corruption. She was happy to let Zardari handle the contracts and business of government. She focused on trying to bring changes to Pakistan, not on how the money was spent. But her reputation as a leader was damaged.

In the next elections, the PPP lost nearly all of its seats in the National Assembly. For two years, Bhutto stayed in Pakistan and tried to defend herself and her husband. But in 1999, she and Zardari were sentenced to five years in prison for corruption. Zardari was imprisoned, but Bhutto left Pakistan for a London visit two days before the verdict. ✑

9 LOOKING FORWARD, LOOKING BACK

Chapter

In an interview in 2000, Benazir Bhutto looked back at her life. She acknowledged that she had made mistakes while governing, but she learned from them. She knew Pakistan had always had problems with corruption in the government, but at the time she was prime minister, it did not seem as important as the violence in the streets or the poverty of the people. Looking back, she said, "I wish I had tackled the so-called corruption issues more deeply." She wonders whether she might still be working in Pakistan if she had paid attention to government corruption right away.

But Bhutto has many enemies in Pakistan who believe that she knew about the corruption. They claim that she and Zardari grew rich on the money

Pakistanis rally in support of ousted Prime Minister Benazir Bhutto.

she stole from Pakistan. Zardari was accused of taking bribes and pocketing money from government contracts. She is accused of using the money to buy expensive jewelry and a house in England.

Whether the corruption charges are true or not, Bhutto cannot return to Pakistan until her name is cleared. Today she lives in England and Dubai, in the United Arab Emirates with her son and daughters, Bakhtawar and Asifa. Her husband was finally released from prison in December 2004 and now lives with his family in exile.

Bhutto enjoys a more relaxed life in England with her family.

Bhutto enjoys the time she spends with her family, but as she says, "My personal happiness has always been subordinated to the greater happiness of the 150 million people of Pakistan." And so she continues to be active in issues of peace and human rights. She keeps a busy schedule of appearances and speeches. Though in self-exile from Pakistan, she continues to travel throughout the rest of South Asia, where she has been given a number of honorary degrees, fellowships, and awards.

Bhutto has not given up on democracy in Pakistan. She remains optimistic that someday democratic elections will be held again. If the current president of Pakistan, General Pervez Musharraf, changes his mind and allows free elections, Bhutto hopes to return to her homeland. If she cannot run for office, she will help the Pakistan People's Party continue the fight for human rights and democracy.

A recent earthquake that devastated her country in October 2005 has given Bhutto hope for

Pervez Musharraf (1943–), the president of Pakistan in 2005, has been a military man all his life. He attended Pakistan Military Academy, and became an officer in 1964. Just one year later, he fought in the war between India and Pakistan. He received medals for his heroism. He rose through the ranks to become general and army chief of staff in 1998. In 1999, he took over the government from Prime Minister Nawaz Sharif. He announced that new elections would not be held until law and order returned to Pakistan. In 2005, he refused to allow Benazir Bhutto to return to Pakistan.

Bhutto attended the Women in Business International Forum with the wife of the Turkish prime minister in 2005.

change—and hope for her return to Pakistan. The government's response to the disaster has been heavily criticized, and Bhutto, who has set up a relief fund for earthquake victims, is now being urged to return. Until that time comes, however, Benazir Bhutto continues her struggles from abroad. She has dedicated her life to fighting for Pakistan, and she will continue. When people ask her how she can be optimistic when Pakistan is again under a military dictatorship, she replies that she must continue for her father and mother. "There could be 10 people who are bad," she said in an interview, "but there are 90 people who are good." She believes that her family has fought for the good people of Pakistan, and she must continue that work.

> *Benazir Bhutto and the Pakistan People's Party continue to encourage Pakistan's current government to hold free and open elections. They want Pakistan to move toward a democratic society. The military government, however, continues to delay elections and make laws that prevent Bhutto from returning to Pakistan and running for office.*

Despite her privileged upbringing, Bhutto has had many obstacles in her path. Through imprisonment, exile, and personal tragedy, however, Bhutto has remained committed to her ideals. She has said:

> *In life there are challenges, but I think leadership is very much predicated on the capacity to absorb defeat and overcome it. Now, after having been in politics for more than two decades, I have come to the strong conclusion that the differ-*

*Though in
exile, Bhutto
still has many
supporters in
Pakistan.*

ence between somebody who succeeds and
somebody who fails is the ability to absorb
a setback.

Her achievements, especially in the face of
devastating setbacks, have inspired young women
all over the world. In a 2000 interview, Bhutto said
that her election to the position of prime minister
"was a victory for women everywhere." Her success
has motivated young women around the world to
strive for leadership roles in their countries and
governments. And though she never planned

to become a role model, her commitment to the ideals of democracy and human rights has influenced the lives of many people of both genders.

Bhutto knows how difficult life can be. Still, she has great hope for the future. She hopes for:

> *a world of peace that provides people opportunities to prosper. Each individual is given life once to lead, and each individual deserves a chance to succeed. ... People need peace and they need opportunity, in Pakistan and everywhere else. That's the world I'd like to see.*

Benazir Bhutto has written two books, Foreign Policy in Perspective *(1978) and* Daughter of Destiny *(1989), her autobiography. Many of her speeches have been collected and published in book form, and she has contributed essays and articles to numerous books and magazines. She continues to actively speak and write on behalf of political and human rights issues.*

Benazir Bhutto will always speak out against violence, injustice, and abuses of human rights. She hopes that someday soon we will all live in a better world—one with equal rights for everyone, including women, the poor, and especially the people of Pakistan.

BHUTTO'S LIFE

1953

Born on June 21 in
Karachi, Pakistan

1965

India and Pakistan go
to war over Kashmir

1967

Father founds
Pakistan People's
Party

1950

1953

The first Europeans
climb Mount Everest

1966

The National
Organization for
Women (NOW) is
established to work
for equality between
women and men

WORLD EVENTS

1968

Father imprisoned for the first time

1969–1973

Studies at Radcliffe College in Cambridge, Massachusetts

1971

East Pakistan wins independence and becomes Bangladesh

1970

1969

U.S. astronauts are the first humans to land on the moon

1971

The first microprocessor is produced by Intel

BHUTTO'S LIFE

1973–1977
Studies at Oxford
University in England

1977
Father's government
is overthrown by
General Zia ul-Haq

1979
Father is hanged
in prison

1973
Arab oil embargo
creates concerns
about natural
resources

1978
The first test-tube
baby conceived
outside its mother's
womb is born in
Oldham, England

WORLD EVENTS

1984

Released from house arrest to get surgery for a serious ear infection in Europe

1985

Brother Shah Nawaz is murdered in France in July

1986

Returns to Pakistan as the leader of the Pakistan People's Party

1985

1983

The AIDS (acquired immune deficiency syndrome) virus is identified

1986

The U.S. space shuttle *Challenger* explodes, killing all seven astronauts on board

BHUTTO'S LIFE

1987

Marries Asif
Ali Zardari on
December 18

1988–1990

Serves first term as
prime minister

1993–1996

Serves second term
as prime minister

1990

WORLD EVENTS

1990

Political prisoner
Nelson Mandela, a
leader of the anti-
apartheid movement
in South Africa, is
released; Mandela
becomes president of
South Africa in 1994

1994

Genocide of 500,000
to 1 million of the
minority Tutsi group
by rival Hutu people
in Rwanda

1996

Brother Mir is
murdered in Karachi
in September

1999

Leaves Pakistan and
goes into exile in
England and Dubai

2004

Husband Asif is
released from prison
in Pakistan after
eight years

2000

1996

A sheep is cloned
in Scotland

2001

Terrorist attacks on
the two World Trade
Center towers in New
York City and
on the Pentagon
in Washington, D.C.,
leave thousands dead

2005

Major earth-
quake kills
thousands in
Pakistan

DATE OF BIRTH: June 21, 1953

BIRTHPLACE: Karachi, Pakistan

FATHER: Zulfikar Ali Bhutto
(1928–1979)

MOTHER: Nusrat Ispahani (1929–)

EDUCATION: Convent of Jesus and
Mary in Karachi, Pakistan
(1958–1968)

Radcliffe College
(1969–1973)

Oxford University,
England (1973–1977)

SPOUSE: Asif Ali Zardari (1956–)

**DATE OF
MARRIAGE:** December 18, 1987

CHILDREN: Bilawal (1988–)
Bakhtawar (1990–)
Asifa (1993–)

FURTHER READING

Anderson, Mercedes Padrino. *Benazir Bhutto*. Philadelphia, Pa.: Chelsea House Publishing, 2004.

Crompton, Samuel Willard. *Pakistan*. Philadelphia, Pa.: Chelsea House Publishers, 2003.

Richardson, Hazel. *Life in the Ancient Indus River Valley*. New York: Crabtree Publishing Company, 2005.

Thimmesh, Catherine. *Madam President: The Extraordinary, True (and Evolving) Story of Women in Politics*. Boston: Houghton Mifflin Company, 2004.

LOOK FOR MORE SIGNATURE LIVES
BOOKS ABOUT THIS ERA:

Fidel Castro: *Leader of Communist Cuba*
ISBN 0-7565-1580-7

Winston Churchill: *British Soldier, Writer, Statesman*
ISBN 0-7565-1582-3

Jane Goodall: *Legendary Primatologist*
ISBN 0-7565-1590-4

Adolf Hitler: *Dictator of Nazi Germany*
ISBN 0-7565-1589-0

Queen Noor: *American-born Queen of Jordan*
ISBN 0-7565-1595-5

Eva Peròn: *First Lady of Argentina*
ISBN 0-7565-1585-8

Joseph Stalin: *Dictator of the Soviet Union*
ISBN 0-7565-1597-1

On the Web

For more information on *Benazir Bhutto*, use FactHound.

1. Go to *www.facthound.com*
2. Type in a search word related to this book or this book ID: 0756515785
3. Click on the *Fetch It* button.

FactHound will fetch the best Web sites for you.

Historic Sites

Asia Society and Museum
725 Park Avenue
New York, NY 10021
212/288-6400
Exhibits provide information on all Asian countries and include an interactive timeline of Asian history.

United Nations
First Avenue and 46th Street
New York, NY 10017
212/963-8687
The United Nations is the meeting place for nearly 200 countries.

cease-fire
an agreement in war in which both sides agree to stop fighting for a period of time

corruption
when people behave dishonestly, especially in government

dictator
a person who completely controls a country, usually ruling unjustly

ethnic
relating to a group of people who share a common race, language, and culture

exile
a condition in which a person is sent away from his or her country, without permission to return

Islam
a religion based on the teachings of the Prophet Muhammad

Koran
the holy book of Islam

martial law
a situation in which the military takes over a government and suspends constitutional laws

Muslim
a person who believes in Islam

shalwar kamiz
traditional Pakistani clothing—usually a long tunic over baggy pants

tear gas
a chemical that makes the eyes burn, often used to stop a riot

Source Notes

Chapter 1

Page 10, line 15: Mary Anne Weaver. *Pakistan: In the Shadow of Jihad and Afghanistan.* New York: Farrar, Straus and Giroux, 2002, p. 190.

Page 13, line 8: "Benazir Bhutto Interview." *Academy of Achievement.* Oct. 27, 2000. 17 November 2005 <http://www.achievement.org/autodoc/page/bhu0int-1>

Chapter 2

Page 18, line 14: Benazir Bhutto. *Daughter of Destiny.* New York: Simon and Schuster, 1989, pp. 36–37.

Page 19, line 5: Ibid., p. 38.

Page 21, line 1: Ibid., p. 44.

Page 22, line 18: "Benazir Bhutto Interview."

Chapter 3

Page 27, line 2: *Daughter of Destiny*, p. 50.

Page 27, line 17: Ibid.

Page 27, line 23: Ibid.

Page 27, sidebar: "Benazir Bhutto Interview."

Page 29, line 23: *Daughter of Destiny*, p. 52.

Page 31, line 7: Ibid., p. 51.

Chapter 4

Page 40, line 1: Ibid., p. 77.

Page 40, line 12: Ibid., p. 80.

Page 40, sidebar: "Benazir Bhutto Interview."

Page 43, line 7: *Daughter of Destiny*, p. 102.

Page 44, line 11: Ibid., p. 18.

Chapter 5

Page 48, line 15: Ibid., p. 162.

Page 50, line 6: Ibid., p. 21.

Page 51, line 16: Ibid., p. 29.

Page 51, sidebar: "Benazir Bhutto Interview."

Page 56, line 4: *Daughter of Destiny*, p. 202.

Chapter 6

Page 61, line 10: Ibid., p. 258–259.

Page 67, line 10: Ibid., p. 331.

Chapter 7

Page 69, line 3: Ibid., p. 325.

Page 70, line 7: Ibid., p. 326.

Chapter 8

Page 83, sidebar: "Press Conference on Pakistan Nuclear Tests." May 29, 1998. 17 November 2005 <http:// nuclearweaponarchive.org/Pakistan/ SharifAnnounce.txt>

Chapter 9

Page 89, line 8: "Benazir Bhutto Interview."

Page 91, line 2: Ibid.

Page 93, line 12: Ibid.

Page 93, line 23: Ibid.

Page 94, line 7: Ibid.

Page 95, line 8: Ibid.

Bhutto, Benazir. *Daughter of Destiny*. New York: Simon and Schuster, 1989.

"Benazir Bhutto Interview." *Academy of Achievement*. Oct. 27, 2000. 17 November 2005 < http://www.achievement.org/autodoc/page/bhu0bio-1>.

"Pakistan: A Country Study." *Library of Congress*. April 1994. 17 November 2005 <http://lcweb2.loc.gov/frd/cs/pktoc.html#pk0128>.

Sinkler, Adrian, ed. *Pakistan: The World's Hotspots*. Farmington Hills, Mich.: Greenhaven Press, 2003.

Weaver, Mary Anne. *Pakistan: In the Shadow of Jihad and Afghanistan*. New York: Farrar, Straus and Giroux, 2002.

Ziring, Lawrence. *Pakistan at the Crosscurrent of History*. Oxford, England: Oneworld Publications, 2003.

Afghanistan, 54, 81
airplane hijacking, 53–54
Al-Murtaza, 18, 50, 51, 59, 59
Al-Zulfikar, 53–54
Amnesty International, 63, 64
Arabic, 20
arranged marriages, 16–17, 71, 72, 73
assassinations, 30–31, 54
Awami League, 37
Ayub Khan, Mohammad, 25, 28, 30, 31, 42

Bangladesh, 38. *See also* East Pakistan.
Benenson, Peter, 64
Bhopali, Zahoorul Hasan, 54
Bhutto, Benazir
    on Al-Murtaza, 18
    arrests of, 10, 47, 48, 52–57, 59–60, 70
    birth of, 16
    books by, 18, 95
    campaigning by, 77–78, 79
    on corruption in government, 89
    on danger in politics, 31
    education of, 20, 22, 29, 33–37, 39–42
    in England, 39–42, 61–64, 65–66
    in exile, 13, 87, 89–95
    on father, 10, 22, 48
    father's career wishes for, 40
    father's death and, 50–52
    father's death sentence and, 47–50
    health of, 54, 60–62, 73–74
    home life of, 27
    importance of, 9–10, 94–95
    importance of religion to, 55–56
    interest in politics of, 27–29
    marriage of, 71–75
    on Mohenjo-daro, 18–19
    nickname of, 18
    opposition to, 11–12, 13
    on poor people, 27
    pregnancy of, 77–78, 79
    as prime minister, 9–10, 80–83, 84–87
    on protests, 40
    religious training of, 20, 21–22, 34
    return to Pakistan by, 69–71
    struggle for democracy by, 10, 50, 51, 67, 81
    on successful people, 93–94
    in United States, 34–37, 39–40
    on women in Islam, 21
Bhutto, Mir Murtaza (brother), 18, 60, 74, 85–86
Bhutto, Nusrat (mother), 16, 17, 21–22, 29, 30, 34, 44, 47, 50, 51–53, 54, 55, 56, 59–60, 85–86
Bhutto, Sanam (sister), 18, 20, 22–23, 27–28, 53, 56, 61, 67
Bhutto, Shah Nawaz (brother), 18, 60–61, 66
Bhutto, Zulfikar Ali (father), 10, 12–13, 16–17, 22, 25–27, 28–31, 33, 37–40, 42–45, 47–51
Britain, 15, 23, 39–42, 61–64, 65–66, 73
Bush, George H.W., 82

Cambridge, Massachusetts, 33
clothing, 17, 34
college, 13, 33–37, 39–42
Convent of Jesus and Mary, 20
corruption in government, 83, 87, 89–90
Council on Foreign Relations, 65

Daughter of Destiny (Benazir
    Bhutto), 18, 95

earthquake, 91–93
East Pakistan, 15, 37–38
education, 17, 20, 22, 29, 33–37,
    39–42
elections, 9, 37–38, 64–65, 77–79,
    80, 84, 93
England, 15, 23, 39–42, 61–64,
    65–66, 73
European Parliament, 65

Foreign Policy in Perspective
    (Benazir Bhutto), 95
Gandhi, Indira, 39
government, 9, 10, 36–38, 39, 64–65,
    77–79, 81, 83, 84, 87, 89–90, 93
government, military in, 13, 31,
    43–44, 78–79, 84, 93
government, religion in, 85
government, women in, 10, 39
Ghulam Ishaq Khan, 79

India, 15, 22–23, 25, 37, 39, 54, 83,
    91
Iran, 17
Islam, burial traditions in, 50, 66–67
Islam, prayer rituals in, 21–22, 34
Islam, sacred book of, 20, 33–34
Islam, sects of, 20
Islam, women in, 11–12, 17, 21, 34,
    71, 81
Islamabad, Pakistan, 9, 42, 81
Islamic Republic of Pakistan, 9
Ispahani, Nusrat. *See* Bhutto, Nusrat
    (mother).

Jinnah, Mohammed Ali, 15
Karachi, Pakistan, 16, 18, 22, 27, 29,
    42, 44–45, 47, 59, 60, 70, 75

Karachi Central Jail, 53, 57, 59
Kashmir, 22–23, 25
Koran, 20, 33–34

Lahore, Pakistan, 29–30
languages, 18, 20
literacy, 31
London, England, 61–64, 73

marriage, 16–17, 56, 71–75
military, 13, 31, 43–44, 78–79, 84, 93
Mohenjo-daro, 18–19
Murree, Pakistan, 22–23, 44
Musharraf, Pervez, 79, 91
Muslim burial traditions, 50, 66–67
Muslim League, 15, 83
Muslim prayer rituals, 21–22, 34
Muslim sacred book, 20, 33–34
Muslim sects, 20
Muslim women, 11–12, 17, 21, 34,
    71, 81

National Assembly, 37–38, 77, 79,
    80, 81, 83, 84
nuclear weapons, 82–83

Oxford University, 39–42

Pakistan, 9, 15, 38, 79
Pakistan International Airlines, 53
Pakistan People's Party (PPP), 9, 10,
    26, 27–31, 37, 80, 87, 93
parliamentary system, 79
Pinkie, 18
poor people, 27, 31
prayer, 21–22
presidential guard, 9
purdah, 17

Radcliffe College, 33–37, 39, 40
Rawalpindi, Pakistan, 42, 47, 48

shalwar kamiz, 9, 34
Sharif, Nawaz, 83–84, 87, 91
Shiite Muslims, 20
South Asia, 10
Sukkur, Pakistan, 53–56
Sunni Muslims, 20
Switzerland, 60

United Nations, 25, 38
United States, 34–37, 39–40, 65,
    82, 84

veils, 17
Vietnam War, 40
wars, 22–23, 25, 37–38, 91

weddings, 56, 74–75
West Pakistan, 15, 37–38
women in government, 10, 39
women in Islam, 11–12, 17, 21, 34,
    71, 81
women's movement, 40

Yahya Khan, 31, 37

Zardari, Asif Ali (husband), 72–75,
    87, 89–90
Zardari, Bilawal (son), 79–80
Zia ul-Haq, Muhammad, 43–45, 47,
    48, 52, 53–54, 57, 62–65, 67,
    69–70, 77, 78

Mary Englar is a freelance writer and a teacher of English and creative writing. She has a master of fine arts degree in writing from Minnesota State University, and has written more than 30 nonfiction books for children. She continues to read and write about the many different cultures of our world in Minnesota.

Image Credits